DOGS HELPING PEOPLE

Sled Dogs
Speeding Through Snow

Alice B. McGinty

The Rosen Publishing Group's
PowerKids Press™
New York

Published in 1999 by The Rosen Publishing Group, Inc.
29 East 21st Street, New York, NY 10010

First Edition

Book Design: Michael de Guzman

Photo Credits: Cover © Robert Winslow/Viesti Associates; p. 4 © Orion/International Stock; p. 7, 8 © H. A. Roberts; p. 11, 15 © Robert Winslow/Viesti Associates, Inc.; p. 12 © B Von Hoffman/H. A. Roberts; p.16 © P. Roter/H. A. Roberts; p. 19 © Archive Photos; p. 20 © Bob Firth/International Stock.

McGinty, Alice B.
   Sled dogs: speeding through snow / by Alice B. McGinty.
      p.   cm. — (Dogs helping people)
   Includes index.
   Summary: Explores the nature and work of sled dogs, what kinds of breeds make sled dogs, and the history of dogsled racing.
   ISBN 0-8239-5216-9
   1. Sled dogs—Juvenile literature. 2. Sled dogs—Alaska—Juvenile literature.
   [1. Sled dogs. 2. Sled dog racing.] I. Title. II. Series.
SF428.7.M34   1997
636.73—dc21
                                              97-45034
                                                    CIP
                                                     AC

Manufactured in the United States of America

Contents

Pups Are Born

Surprise! A group of **malamute** (MAL-uh-myoot) puppies have been born. Their mother cleans them, feeds them, and keeps them warm.

Someone else is watching over the pups too. Jill, their owner, picks them up and holds them several times each day.

She wants the pups to get used to her smell. She also wants them to feel comfortable around people.

When these pups grow up, they will pull a dogsled. And Jill will teach them how to do it. Their safety and their lives will depend on each other.

▽ *A group of puppies born at the same time from the same mother is called a litter.*

A Sled Dog's History

Sled dogs have helped people for thousands of years. People in the far North depended on dogsleds to travel over ice and snow. The dogsleds carried supplies and followed animals during hunts.

America discovered sled dogs during the Gold Rush of the 1800s. During this time, many people from America moved to land that is now the state of Alaska, hoping to find gold there. Like the Alaskan **natives** (NAY-tivz), Americans needed dogsleds to get around. When there was no snow, sled dogs carried supplies in backpacks.

Arctic explorers used sled dogs to carry their supplies as they traveled. ▷

Pulling

A special person must teach the dogs, take care of them, and drive the dogsled. That person is called a **musher** (MUSH-er). The word "musher" comes from a French word that means "to walk."

It's not hard to teach a sled dog to pull something. Sled dogs naturally love to pull! Their strong bodies and big feet are made for pulling. Mushers hook sled dog pups into soft **harnesses** (HAR-nes-ez) that are tied to small logs. The pups run, pulling the logs. This way, they get used to pulling something behind them.

◁ *Not only do sled dogs love to pull, they also enjoy being outside in cold, snowy weather.*

Learning Commands

Many mushers take both their older dogs and the pups on long hikes for exercise. The pups see the older dogs obeying the musher's commands. In this way, the pups learn to obey too. To teach the pups, the musher guides a harnessed pup to the left. "**Haw**" (HAW), he says. That is the command to turn left. The pups also learn "**Gee**" (JEE) to turn right, and "**Whoa**" (WOH) to stop.

Dogsleds have no reins for steering. Instead, the musher shouts commands that tell the dogs when to stop, go, or turn.

Sled dogs listen for commands from their master that tell them which way to go. ▷

Picking the Team

Mushers, like coaches, want to pick the best dogs for their sled teams. There are many types of sled dogs. **Siberian huskies** (sy-BEER-ee-un HUS-keez), **Samoyeds** (sam-OY-yedz), and **Inuit** (IH-new-it), or Eskimo dogs, are all popular **breeds** (BREEDZ). These breeds are smaller and faster than malamutes. Like all sled dogs, they have thick fur to keep them warm in the cold.

Each dog has a different **personality** (PER-suh-NAL-ih-tee) too. Who will be a good leader? Who runs hardest? Which dogs get along? A good musher knows the answers.

◁ *These Siberian husky pups can grow as big as 80 pounds.*

Hitching Up

It's time to pull the dogsled! The musher harnesses the dogs. He attaches a long rope, called a gang line, to the sled. He hooks two lead dogs up front. The lead dogs must be smart. Their job is to guide the team.

The musher hooks another pair of older dogs behind the leaders. Then he hooks two pups behind them. The pups will learn as they follow the older dogs.

When there is no snow, the dogs pull a three-wheeled cart as part of their training.

This way of arranging the dogs is called a Gang Hitch. ▷

"Hike!"

The dogs bark excitedly as they are harnessed. "Hike!" calls the musher. And off they go! The musher balances himself on the sled's **runners** (RUN-erz). The team trots along the trail. "Gee!" calls the musher. The team turns right.

When it gets cold, the musher runs next to the sled for a little while to stay warm. The dogs pull faster. Cold weather keeps them moving.

Suddenly, the puppies try to chase a rabbit. They get tangled in their ropes. The musher stops and untangles them. She patiently teaches the pups to stay on the trail.

◁ *Sled dogs learn to work with their master as a team.*

17

The Race for Life

In 1925 sled dogs saved a town! In Nome, Alaska, many people got sore throats and high fevers. They had **diphtheria** (dip-THEER-ee-uh). But the town doctor did not have enough medicine. If he didn't get more medicine quickly, many people would die.

The fastest way to bring the medicine to Nome was by dogsled. Different towns asked their best mushers and dogs to form a **relay** (REE-lay). Brave teams traveled day and night through a terrible blizzard. In five and a half days, they had traveled 674 miles and delivered the medicine. Nome was saved!

18

In New York City's Central Park there is a statue of Balto, the lead sled dog who ▷ carried the medicine into Nome.

The Iditarod Trail Sled Dog Race

In honor of the 1925 Race for Life, Alaskans organized a sled dog race called the **Iditarod** (eye-DIT-er-od) Trail Sled Dog Race. The native word iditarod means "distant place."

The Iditarod Trail used to be a dogsled mail route. Today the trail is part of the world's longest sled dog race. Each spring, mushers from all over the world travel to Alaska. They race over 1,100 miles from Anchorage to Nome through icy winds and temperatures below −40°. The fastest racers reach Nome in about ten days.

◁ *Each night, racers and their dogs set up camps along the trail where they rest until the next morning.*

Sled Dogs Today

Many jobs that used to be done by sled dogs are now done by airplanes and snowmobiles. But in some places people still use dogsleds to travel and hunt. Rangers in Alaska's Danali National Park use dogsleds to patrol areas of the park that snowmobiles can't reach.

Many people raise and train sled dogs for fun. They explore. They give sightseeing rides on the sleds. They also have dogsled races. Like Jill and her pups, mushers and dogs work together to do what neither could do alone.

Glossary

breed (BREED) A group of animals that are related and are very much alike.

diphtheria (dip-THEER-ee-uh) A serious illness of the throat.

gee (JEE) The command to turn right.

harness (HAR-nes) A strap worn by a sled dog that hooks onto a sled.

haw (HAW) The command to turn left.

iditarod (eye-DIT-er-od) An Alaskan word meaning distant place.

Inuit (IH-new-it) **dog** A type of sled dog known for being able to handle cold weather.

malamute (MAL-uh-myoot) A type of large sled dog.

musher (MUSH-er) The driver of a dogsled.

native (NAY-tiv) A person who was born, grew up, and lives in one place.

personality (PER-suh-NAL-ih-tee) How a person or animal acts and relates to others.

relay (REE-lay) When something is passed along in stages from one team to another.

runner (RUN-er) One of the flat, narrow pieces on which a sled slides.

Samoyed (sam-OY-yed) A type of sled dog with thick white fur.

Siberian husky (sy-BEER-ee-un HUS-kee) A type of sled dog with short hair.

whoa (WOH) The command to stop.

Index